Happy Halloween
TRY IF YOU CAN TO GET
ALL THE CORRECT
ANSWERS !!
In this fun &
educational
book

THIS BOOK
BELONGS TO :

I Spy with my Little eye
something beginning with
A

A is for Angel

I Spy with my Little eye
something beginning with
B

B is for Bat

I Spy with my Little eye
something beginning with
"C"

C is for Candy

I Spy with my Little eye
something beginning with
"D"

D is for Devil

I Spy with my Little eye something beginning with

E is for Eyeballs

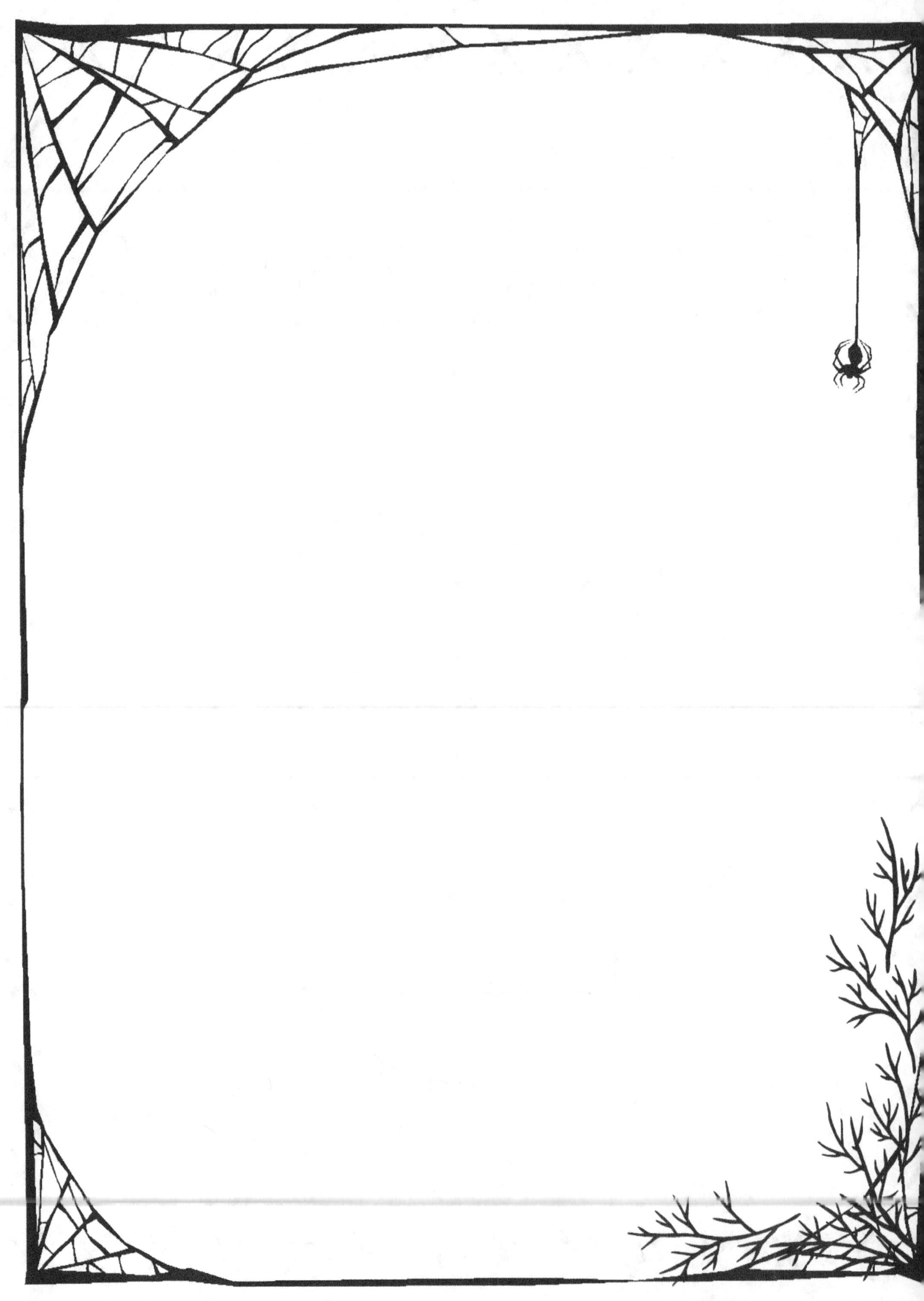

I Spy with my Little eye 👀 something beginning with

F is for Fairy

I Spy with my Little eye
something beginning with
"G"

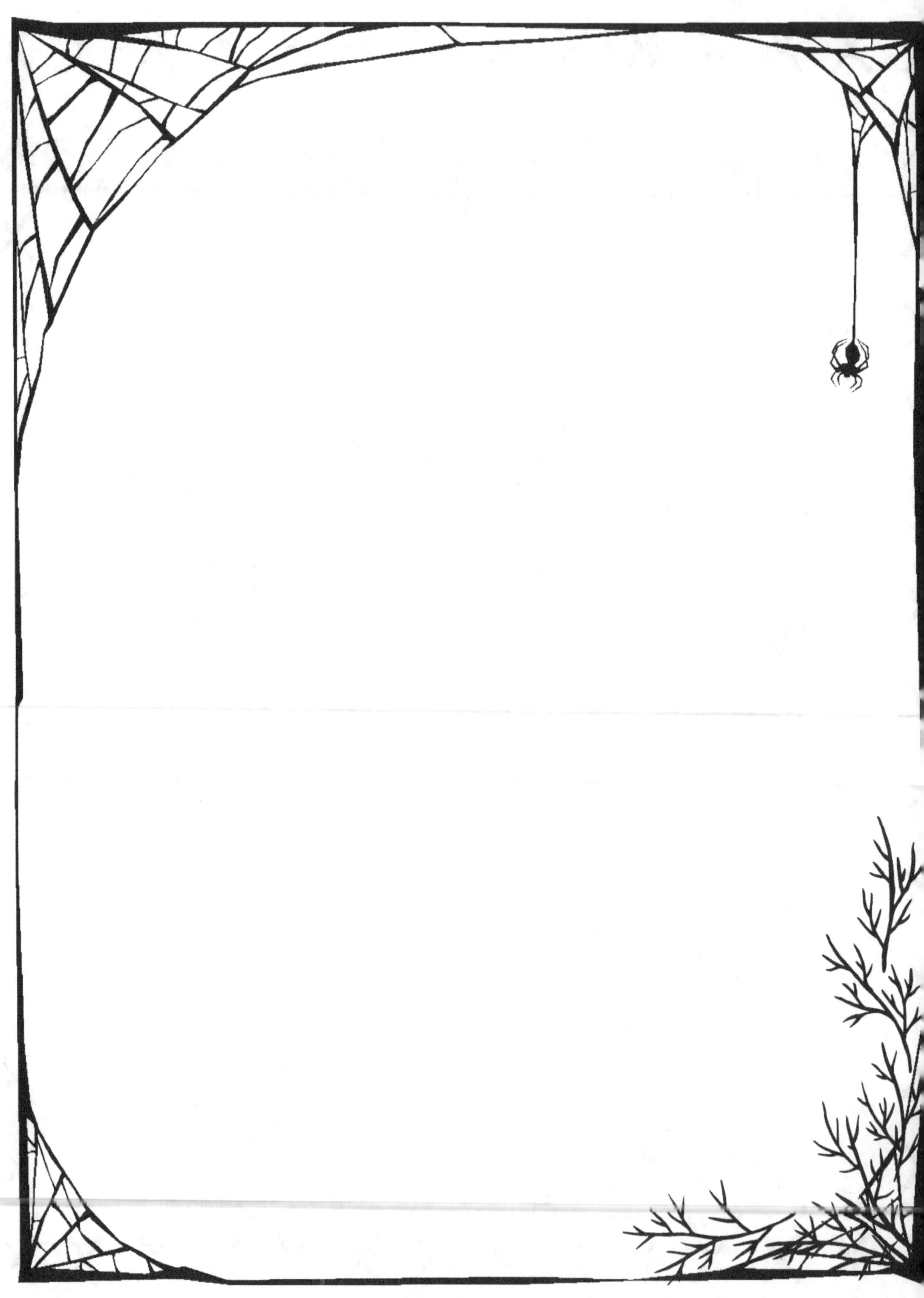

G is for Ghost

I Spy with my Little eye
something beginning with
"   "
H

H is for Haunted
House

I Spy with my Little eye
something beginning with
" I "

I is for Ice-cream

I Spy with my Little eye
something beginning with
"J"

J is for Jar

I Spy with my Little eye
something beginning with
K

K is for King

I Spy with my Little eye 👀 something beginning with

L is for Labyrinth

I Spy with my Little eye
something beginning with
M

M is for Mummy

I Spy with my Little eye
something beginning with
"N"

N is for Ninja

I Spy with my Little eye
something beginning with

O is for Owl

9 798553 758479